THE UNSWEPT PATH

The Unswept Path

Contemporary American Haiku

Edited by
John Brandi and Dennis Maloney

Companions for the Journey, Volume 8

White Pine Press / Buffalo, New York

Acknowledgments:
Michael McClure, "Haiku Edge" and all haiku are from *Rain Mirror,* New
Directions, 1999. Reprinted by permission of New Directions Publishing
Company.

Acknowledgments continue on page 217.

Publication of this book was made possible, in part, with public funds
from the New York State Council on the Arts, a State Agency.

Printed and bound in the United States of America.

First Edition

Library of Congress Control Number: 2005929022

Companions for the Journey Series, volume 8

Published by
White Pine Press
P.O. Box 236
Buffalo, New York 14201
www.whitepine.org

Dedicated to the Memory of

Cid Corman
Elizabeth Searle Lamb

"Don't follow the steps of the ancients;
seek what they sought."
—Matsuo Bashô

Contents

PREFACE

The Unswept Path: Contemporary American Haiku includes a greater variety of English-language haiku than any other book I can think of, now some hundred years after poets of Europe and the Americas discovered haiku and fifty years after the beginnings of a haiku movement in North America. Together, these poets move decisively beyond any particular camp boundaries that may enclose one or another group of haiku writers. As Edith Shiffert says so clearly, "Haiku poets, as all poets, should feel free to use the haiku in whatever way seems appropriate to their creativity. There never were any rules, just fashions and preferences."

Here, encounter three established leaders of the American haiku community, poets who have concentrated most of their efforts on haiku, and who consciously expand the understanding of older Japanese haiku developed in the mid-twentieth century by such commentators as R. H. Blyth, Harold G. Henderson, and Kenneth Yasuda. Christopher Herold writes richly Zen-imbued haiku. William J. Higginson offers alternating images of inner and outer worlds. Elizabeth Searle Lamb shares the minute daily revelations in her life. Along with them, find two poets who discovered haiku in the nexus of the Beat Generation and San Francisco poets, following the lead of Gary Snyder, Allen Ginsberg, and Jack Kerouac, but soon moved on to create their own new and striking poems. Enter the crystalline snapshots of the mind by Diane DiPrima and the reimagined animal songs of Michael McClure.

Not surprisingly, several poets in *The Unswept Path* began their work in the genre while living and studying for long periods in Japan, and present another varied tapestry of what haiku in English can be. Margaret Chula's delicately precise verses evince a deep assimilation of Japanese cultural practices developed during a dozen years in Kyôto. Cid Corman's aphoristic, almost gnomic, verses in this collection illustrate much of the range of his longer poetry. And Edith Shiffert contributes her objective and yet warmly human verses embedded in a clear-as-light essay on aging in a foreign land. Both Corman and Shiffert have spent a majority of their adult lives in Japan.

Like Corman, DiPrima, and McClure, many of the poets here have made substantial names for themselves outside the small world of haiku. What reader first thinks of John

Brandi, Patricia Donegan, Penny Harter, Sonia Sanchez, or Steve Sanfield as "a haiku poet"? Yet many of Brandi's travel-books of poems and essays include clusters of his sharply piquant haiku. Donegan, known for several collections of longer poems and as a teacher of poetry at Naropa Institute, actually studied haiku under a leading Japanese master, Seishi Yamaguchi, and has co-authored an important book on Japanese haiku, but her own haiku ring with the authority of a self-developed poet. Harter, well known for the often mysterious connecting leaps in her haiku, is better known for her numerous collections of long poems; she recently received the William O. Douglas Nature Writing Award for a group of them. Sanchez brings to haiku the special blend of wisdom, eroticism, and lyricism that makes hers a leading voice among African-American poets. And Sanfield's appearance here as an erotic haiku poet (or two?) can only add to his expanding reputation as both multi-cultural storyteller and American Zennist extraordinaire.

Why bring these poets together in what may seem a confusing welter of diverse voices and ideals too broad to fit under that apparently simple rubric, haiku? To demonstrate that "haiku" may have too many faces to appreciate it fully from only one point of view. These poets may agree with one or another on some basic ideas about haiku—as seen in their useful and varied introductory essays. But each poet has also worked the territory of haiku into a personal landscape; here they offer strikingly different panoramas of image and sound, joy and sadness, recollection and thought.

With *The Unswept Path,* American haiku nods graciously to its Japanese roots, but also claims its place as a full-grown member of the family of American poetry.

—William J. Higginson
Summit, New Jersey
Thanksgiving 2004

John Brandi

Trigger of Light

I live in the spare, high desert of the American Southwest, a land of apparent and often illusory emptiness, a blinding bowl of light that triggers one to write with an economy of words. The eye follows winding arroyos, lizard tracks, and blowing seed. The breath gathers momentum along ridges, faults, and prehistoric waterlines. Fossils scatter at the feet, clay shards glisten after a sudden rain. With the sun's return, the abstract configurations and anthropomorphic designs on the shards dry into muted colors. Pinched fingerprints in the clay reveal the hands of a vanished artisan. I am reminded of

Sappho's poems. Fragments, mysterious and striking to the eye. Missing something essential, but somehow made more essential because of what's missing.

If I'm in the right state of openness—intellect absent, the world before me as is, no hint of another to come—then poems arrive unexpectedly, as they should. After a moment of surprise, a blink of wonder, a little shift in reality, I often scribble a line or two. Eventually my pocket pad brightens with a trail of stepping stones that gets me across the larger waters of heavy thought, mundane practicalities, emotional sidetracks. Haiku are temporary footholds in the stream's middle. They provide balance, keep us spontaneous, allow for the next step without thinking. Each stone shines like a mirror, triggering light into the larger, darker mind. What the big mind doesn't see, the little one does:

> that fallen flower
> returning to the branch
> was a butterfly.
>
> (Moritake)

During instances of awe, when seer and seen are interdependent, we are in the ring, knocked out. After the count, we rise, eyes blinking, the world rearranged. Something familiar has taken on a peculiar significance, void of meaning, filled with delight. Haiku is a deliverance. It shows us, like R.H. Blyth pointed out, "what we knew all the time but did not know we knew." This knocked-out surprise and the resulting poem is not always so dramatic, of course. The magic of Bashô's

> old pond
> a frog jumps in
> —splash!

is that readers have had endless takes on the poem over the centuries. Bashô's slippery creature of both worlds is caught in the act of disappearing while at the same time creating a lasting ripple. It becomes soundless while simultaneously leaving a sound. The frog isn't on a lily pad singing as it had been for countless decades in thousands of traditional Japanese haiku. It is taking a plunge, getting dirty. "My frog is going to disappear from all these frog poems that have been with us too long," Bashô implies. "He is leaving. Now we can write about other things." The frog breaks the rules. Bashô jumps right in after him. What's left?

> a bat flying
> willow to willow
> in the evening glow.
> (Kikaku)

My introduction to haiku came during my late teens, long after my parents provided me with enough early ventures into the natural world to set the background. Browsing Chinatown in Los Angeles one summer, I discovered—in a dim sandalwood-scented shop full of antique scrolls—a book by D. T. Suzuki: *Zen and Japanese Culture*. It was a substantial hardback printed on milky paper with a hefty scattering of illustrations: brush-painted tigers, peach trees in snow, monkeys peering from bamboo, cloud-hidden retreats of mendicants, a solitary angler in whirling mist. In the dark clutter of the shop, incense smoldered in a sun ray. A cat napped under a lacquered red altar set with a cup of tea and two tangerines. On the wall were antique photos of family elders. The world was suddenly very old, and very new. With eager adventure, I purchased the book, the most I'd ever spent on the printed word, and began to devour its contents. As I drifted in and out of many striking passages, one remained with me, from a chapter titled "Love of Nature":

Heaven and earth and I are of the same root,
The ten-thousand things and I are of one substance . . .

Those words evoked my exact boyhood feeling when standing in a lost grove of sun-filtered giant sequoias in the Sierra Nevada. Even then, without being able to define it as such, the moment was religious. I was raised as a Catholic, but the mystery I felt while chanting Latin or swinging a censer of incense before a candle-lit icon, did not match the uplift, the unmeasurable mystery of oneness, that overpowered me in the redwoods.

Suzuki wrote about the gap between the eye and what the eye sees. To be human is to be stuck with a mind relentlessly filling that gap with definition, categorization, empirical analysis, the need to make sense. He said that the myriad forms of heaven and earth, ourselves included, are part of an identical root, a root that "must be firmly seized upon so that there is an actual experience of it." People looking at a flower, for example, essentially remain apart from the flower. "They have no firm hold, they are as if dreaming of a flower. The one who beholds is separated from the object which is beheld." To let go of the subjective ego is to experience the essence of the flower, rather than the counterfeit flower produced by the mind. In so defining this process, Suzuki prepared me for what was to be the most important chapter in the book, "Zen and Haiku." In it was a poem by Masaoka Shiki (1869–1902):

> among the grasses
> an unknown flower
> blooming white.

I had seen that flower, lost in a meadow, high in the sunlit grasses above the middle fork of the Kaweah River. It was insignificant, nameless. It was everything. As I pressed my eye toward it on hands and knees, it was every bit as large as a redwood. Lost in its whiteness, I was inseparable from it. At that instant, if the poet in me had been at work, my task would have been to net the jewel of that oneness, that feeling of is-ness. Then I read Suzuki's footnote:

The human mind is generally found to be chock-full of ideas and concepts. When a man sees a flower he sees clustered with it all kinds of associated analytical thoughts, and it is not the flower in its suchness. It is only when prajña-intuition is exercised that "the flower is red and the willow is green."

Prajña-intuition might be defined as that singular moment when we are at one with the things of the world, receiving them naturally, unhindered. Just as the mind does not stop to analyze each of our 23,000 daily breaths, neither does it stop to analyze the flower. It does not go to a botanical text for names, compare the flower to a star, contrast it with a redwood tree, or seek a metaphor in the apparent loneliness of the flower and the emotional state of the perceiver (how can a flower be lonely?). Mind isn't, flower is. Experience is primary, intellectual size-up is residue. Analysis can be done in a laboratory with the specimen plucked and dead, but it shouldn't happen down on our knees in a meadow. Nor should the fingers be busy counting syllables. The haiku is already written before the hand picks up the pen. It is in the breath, carried for a while like a song, a gift originating not from the muse, but from flower and self as one.

Matsuo Bashô (1644–1694) put it this way:

What is important is to keep your mind high in the world of true understanding, yet not to forget the value of the low. Seek always the truth of beauty, but always return to the world of common experience. Learn about the pine only from the pine, or about the bamboo only from the bamboo. When you see an object, leave your subjective preoccupation with yourself; otherwise you impose yourself on the object, and do not learn.

Along with Suzuki, I read Muir, Whitman, and Thoreau. But Suzuki's ideas were so overwhelming that all I could do was put down the book, lie back, and be impressed that halfway around the planet was a very old and introspective culture that celebrated a way of being in the world with which I identified. Between college art and anthropology, I took a creative writing class, but the professor discouraged haiku, warning that it was an "over-imitated Japanese pastime." Disappointed, I returned to painting, encouraged by artists like Morris Graves, Emily Carr, Albert Ryder, and Hokusai—"Old Man Mad About Drawing." I read with delight the poets Yosa Buson (1716–1783) and Kobayashi Issa (1763–1827), whom I discovered in R. H. Blyth's four-volume *Haiku.* In one of his commentaries, Blyth described haiku as "an expression of a temporary enlightenment in which we see into the life of things," a form having seventeen syllables, a seasonal word *(kigo)*, and a strong sense of place.

Suzuki, Blyth, Hokusai, a few iconoclast painters, and the Japanese haiku masters suited my temperament perfectly. The way they saw the world deeply complimented my increasing forays out of Los Angeles, up the wind-blasted Big Sur coast. A primeval landscape, it was home to artists like Henry Miller, Robinson Jeffers, Jaime de Angulo, Edward Weston, and Emil White. The fog-shrouded cliffs were charged with the deep roll of Asian wind. After spring storms the air was champagne, the hills emerald, the coves sparkling, the mountainous backdrop mottled with blue ceanothus and orange poppies. Once, beach combing, I found a hand-blown glass float from a fishing net washed across the sea from Japan. Eying the horizon, I was convinced I could see the tip of Hokkaido jutting from the fog.

Camped in redwood canyons, I tried a few haiku, but inevitably the dripping trees said it better. Counting syllables, worried whether the *kigo* was there, concerned that my haiku were rigidly dictated by rules not my own, I abandoned the form. Years passed, then two incidents rekindled my flame. First, I discovered the Japanese poet Santôka Taneda (1882–1940), who broke the rules I disliked. His life revealed that wandering was a poetic and spiritual discipline, a way of getting down low, keeping close to the unfettered lives of people at work in nature. It seemed to me that Santôka took to the road like Bashô did, not simply to be "informed" by nature, but to be reformed by it. Second, I met the poet Steve Sanfield, who was living in a cabin in the Sierras and writing his own haiku. What was important, he reminded me, was to show the season of the heart and to realize, like Whitman when he disregarded European influences to embody the new rhythms of his continent, that haiku needn't clone Japanese predecessors in style or content.

The lid was off! I no longer had to be Japanese but could write from where I stood, wept, slept, exalted. I could pursue haiku as the spontaneous leap of nature into my consciousness. Or catch myself bumbling in quick-flash snippets of awkward human folly which the Japanese called *senryu*. At this time, the Japanese poet Issa became a favorite. Blyth referred to him as "the poet of destiny who moved with the movement of fate." Issa brought me down to the little creatures in nature, ones lost among brambles and dewdrops. He wrote about fleas, polywogs, mosquitoes, lice; and himself, the clumsy human who lived among them.

Issa opened up a democratic approach to haiku, took it from the literary circles, put it into the hands of the people. Anyone could write it. Priest, farmer, samurai, prostitute, vagabond, scholar, child, grown-up: all could be moved—despite caste, gender, age, or background—by a moon-white rainbow, a flooded field sparkling with stars, a solitary room darkened by a passing cloud, or little girls fanning goldfish on a hot afternoon. Two haiku by Issa:

> how lovely
> through the torn paper window
> —the Milky Way.

> it begins
> from the cicada's song
> the gentle breeze.

There is a feeling of *sabi* in the first poem, a rustic unpretentiousness coupled with a kind of loneliness. Everything in the universe is celebrated as is: a little ragged around the edges; ungainly; never made perfect by standards of art, yet inexplicably endowed with beauty. A draft through the torn paper window wakes Issa, but he doesn't complain. Instead, he peers through the tear to witness a marvel: the webbed light of the galaxy swimming through space. Standing before the huge expanse of the Milky Way, he is transported from the woes of his humble shack into the beauty of a much larger room. As in Van Gogh's *Starry Night*, everything arrives in an overpowering swirl, then disappears into the evaporative realm of eternal return.

The second poem is fascinating in its turnaround. The breeze, for once, does not carry the insect's song; it is a movement generated by that song. It would take textbooks to explain the pure, mysterious phenomenon of sound creating movement, not only in the ear, but in the universe. The ancient *rishis* of India understood this well, for they could both see and hear sound. Issa, with only a few words, gives us the mystery and the science. But science isn't the point. Whitman, in his notebooks, said: "Bring all the art and science of the world, and baffle and humble it with one spear of grass."

Santôka wrote poems in a spirit similar to Issa's:

> for once
> both the futon and the night
> were long enough.

in the grass
trampled by the horse
flowers in full bloom.

today again
no mail
dragonflies here and there.

The first poem brings a chuckle. Both the length of the night and the length of the bed are at last accommodating. After the chuckle, poignancy creeps in. The poem's bare details reveal much about Santôka's poverty. His life was unadorned; likewise his words. He enjoyed no permanent living quarters or conveniences. He was a wanderer, always between this world and that. As a mendicant, he was often sick and penniless. Perpetually on the move, it is said that Santôka journeyed over 28,000 miles on foot.

His next two poems indicate season by using "flowers in full bloom" and "dragonflies." In the second poem the flowers endure despite the horse tramping the grass. In nature all goes on without blame. Strength, action, passivity, destruction, creation—they exist simultaneously. The third poem powerfully expresses a contrast between empty and full. There is an absence of mail, nothing to hold or read. Yet life is replete, the nonhuman world alive and brimming. The poet sees the hovering dragonflies, and human emotion evanesces. The dragonflies are timeless, transient. As in a *sumi-e* brush painting, they are transparent, elusive.

Such a big world to explore in these small poems. It would take a book, not an essay, to reveal how much is really there when a poet says:

the crane's legs
have gotten shorter
in the spring rain
        (Bashô)

not a single stone
to throw at the dog—
the winter moon
        (Taigi)

just as he is
he goes to bed and gets up
—the snail
        (Issa)

morning glory—
the well-bucket entangled
I ask for water
        (Chiyo-ni)

The poem by Chiyo-ni (1703–1775) exemplifies her compassion. Instead of plucking the flower or removing the vine that has crept around the water-fetching bucket, she halts with a realization: this simple flower is an equal in her world. The morning glory has found an unexpected home in the well, and in her heart. Rather than disturb nature, Chiyo-ni inconveniences herself and borrows water from a neighbor. Her poem paints a picture with hardly a word said, and with no philosophic allusions. Everything is fragile and ephemeral in this world of flowers and humans. Like the flower, we come, we go. A similar recognition of life's impermanence is expressed in the poetry of the Aztecs:

> The body makes a few flowers
> then drops away withered
> somewhere.

We write poems to stay alive, to see where we've been, to give clearing for the next step. A deep surprise, a gong-rattling clonk, a giddy bafflement, a quiet revelation of the mysterious in the everyday: these zaps of primal, uninhibited delight are the seeds of haiku. Often frayed and threadbare, these poems are not concerned with a lasting beauty, but with a significant moment amid everything transient—a split second in which things are profound, yet without meaning. They return us to our dragonfly nature, our morning-glory nature, our heat-of-day nature, our heron-in-the-mist selves:

> clear water
> no front
> no back.
>
> (Chiyo-ni)

Poised for a moment in the extrasensory third eye, these are the poems we live for: ones that explode from a seed, rise on a breeze, fall back to the soil to renew the universe. Full of abandonment, precise in their communication, they are here to be savored as is the full moon on an empty belly. Water seeps through stone as we sleep. A morning breeze begins not only a new day but a new world. A gardenia petal falls to the table during an argument. Long after the raven flies, its shadow stays on the wall. Outside snow falls. Inside the nightgown over the chair is warm. What is familiar is suddenly renewed. The sameness, the difference, are one. Haiku expresses the ineffable magic of this unity. It captures and releases the light of a world that disappears as quickly as it arrives.

I put down the pen, notice spring clouds have darkened. A moist breeze fills the room. On the sandstone path,

> a raindrop.
> Inside it another
> has fallen.

daybreak
pollen rising
from the unswept path

around the bell
blue sky
ringing

late moon
each thought the other
had the key

in the rain
before dawn
snails migrating

last night's dream
wrote it with the wrong end
of the pencil

so broke
size up the porch
for firewood

after the storm
a dragonfly
pinned to the cactus

weightless ridges
my pen
too heavy

about to kill an ant
but no it's carrying
a corpse

a party
where everyone says goodbye
then stays

no romance she warns
and thus plants
the idea

without clothes
it's a different
conversation

morning chill
every haystack leans
to the sun

guests for breakfast
two peonies
and a poppy

not knowing what to say
he mails
only the envelope

wake in a new land
water music
from swaying bamboo

market day
on the prettiest woman
the biggest knife

returning my change
the weaver's
blue hands

after the rain
bomb craters filled
with stars

writing postcards
no mother
no father

fallen leaves
the abbot sweeps
around them

autumn dusk
a bobbing branch
where the crow has flown

the bramble gatherer
lifts her chin
to show the way

old monk
pruning plums
my father's thin arms

between the sound
of the sea
a brass band

thinking of retirement
he realizes
he never had a job

on the pallbearer's feet
the dead man's
shoes

daughter and son grown
their rooms filled
with moonlight

daybreak
coyote's Charlie Parker
impromptu

in the mirror
the old man I was afraid of
as a child

instead of friends
he visits
another mountain

reach the summit
karma
still with me

so cold
naming the stars
to keep warm

all night
listening to the mountain
become water

one man   one fire
snow falling
all day

now that fallen leaves
have buried the path
the trail is clear

Margaret Chula

Tales of a Paper Lantern:
Seasons in a Japanese House

Nearly all my memories of Japan center around a ramshackle wooden house in Kyôto where John and I lived for twelve years. Most modern Japanese would have considered it uninhabitable, but for us it was a sanctuary, a place of quiet harmony and welcome solitude.

If one believes in geomancy, the house was ideally situated at the edge of a hillside which was engraved with the Chinese characters *Myô* and *Hô*, marvelous law of the Buddha. Mt. Hiei was visible from our kitchen window and just outside the back door lay rice paddies and fields of vegetables. Lady Bountiful, the name we gave to our favorite farmlady, peddled her produce from a cart which she pulled through the neighborhood, exchanging gossip along the way.

A two-story wooden structure with a tiled roof, the house measured about 660 square feet. Our main sitting room had eight tatami mats and overlooked a moss garden bordered by pine and camellia trees. We ate our meals seated on tatami, tucking our feet under a *kotatsu* (low table with a heater underneath) in the winter. The focal point was the *tokonoma*, an alcove where a seasonal flower arrangement and scroll were displayed.

Our tiny kitchen accommodated only one person at a time. The appliances were primitive by American standards—a two-burner stove and a refrigerator only three feet high—which necessitated shopping every day. Hot water came from a gas heater over the sink. There were two shelves for dishes and only one drawer.

We slept upstairs on a futon that we rolled up every morning and stored in a closet. One *tansu* held our everyday clothes, and the closet was a rod suspended from the ceiling. Besides the *tansu*, the only other furniture consisted of an antique vanity that I draped my necklaces over. When an earthquake occurred, we would be awakened by the sound of them clanking against the glass.

We took our baths, or rather soaked, in a traditional *ôfuro*, a wooden tub one meter long on each side. But first, we sat on a small stool and ladled water over ourselves to wash. The tub had not been properly maintained, however, and began to leak. By stirring in rice bran, we temporarily plugged the pores. This was not a cheerful room. An artist friend described the color of the walls as elephant's breath. So, when John and I returned from Giverney, we painted our *ôfuro* the same canary yellow as Monet's dining room.

The toilet, a separate room from the bath, could be described as an in-house outhouse. Just large enough to turn around in, it featured a porcelain-rimmed hole in the tiled floor, covered with a wooden lid. Below was a large concrete-lined pit. In his book, *In Praise of Shadows,* Junichiro Tanizaki says: "The Japanese toilet is truly a place of spiritual repose. There are certain prerequisites, a degree of dimness, absolute cleanliness and quiet so complete one can hear the hum of a mosquito. From the window one must have a beautiful sight. The atmosphere should be pleasant, artistically simple but tasteful."

Our toilet was dimly lit. Outside the window, blue morning glories trellised up the fence. After ripping out the urinal in the ante-room, I installed a shelf, covered it with an indigo fabric, and displayed an *ikebana*. In tea ceremony, the flower arrangement has a special name, *chabana* (flowers for tea). Our primitive toilet was called a *benjo*, so we had *benjobana*.

The honey dipper arrived once a month to pump out the pit. In the interim we relied on an electric fan attached to the exhaust stack outside the house to draw out the odor. One sultry day it became obvious that the fan was not doing its job. We discovered that the neighbor's wisteria vine had twined up to our roof, wound itself around the rotating fan, and strangled it!

Spring

Spring begins with rice planting. Behind our house, Lady Bountiful and her husband, Mr. B, usher in the rice cycle by plowing and flooding the fields.

> plowing the paddy
> myna birds marching
> just behind

On an auspicious day, the rice seedlings are taken out of their starting beds and transplanted. Overnight the neighborhood fills with the sound of frogs.

> in strawmat raincoats
> farmers plant rice
> their boots croaking

Cherry blossoms appear in early April. We join our neighbors, strolling along the canal to enjoy their transient beauty.

> last blossoms
> man in a wheelchair
> wheels by slowly

The Japanese say there are four seasons in Japan, but there are actually five. Rainy season, *tsuyu*, is poetically translated as plum rain, reminiscent of green plums seen through new green leaves. In reality, *tsuyu* is a month of stultifying wet heat. Japanese women fan themselves in a frenzy, intoning "*mushi atsui, mushi atsui*" (muggy, muggy) like a Buddhist sutra that will, if repeated often enough, bring relief from suffering. Even the bamboo railings in our old house become slippery. Futons fill with moisture till they compress into soggy lumps. Leather shoes grow furry with mold. During breaks in the rain, we thread our laundry onto a bamboo pole, then hang the pole on wooden supports outside the second-story window. We have no clothes dryer. Futons are laid out on the roof to dry.

> airing the futons
> on the first day of sunshine
>   bulbul fluffs his wings

Insects thrive in the damp heat. Centipedes and ants find their way into the leaks and crevices of our old house. I try to stay cool lying on tatami in a cotton *yukata*. A bouquet of peonies releases its fragrance into the still air.

> all at once
> peony blossoms drop
>   clap of thunder

Ants trail up and down the fallen peony petals and I'm startled to find

> they have discovered
> my flowered kimono
> those relentless ants

Even worse is the *mukade*. A centipede's sting can kill a young child. During *tsuyu, mukade* search out dry, dark places. One day while reaching into the back of the closet, I felt a sharp prick. A six-inch-long centipede had curled itself around my finger!

Cicadas chose this season to appear. After nine years underground, they begin the slow process of emerging from their shells, leaving their ghostly casements still clinging to the branches. Their song is shrill, spikes of sound that resound in the dull heat.

> sawing afternoon
> into evening
> cicadas
>
> cicadas—
> tree root
>   pulses

There is, however, one wonderful thing about the rainy season.

FIREFLY LANTERNS

In early June, we get a telephone call from Murayama-san, our potter friend from Ayabe.

"Maggie," he says, "the fireflies are out!"

"Okay," I say, "we'll be right up!"

Ayabe is a two-and-a-half hour drive from Kyôto along a rural highway that meanders through mountain villages. John and I pack an overnight bag and leave right after our university classes finish. Murayama-san, his wife Ayako, and ten-year-old daughter Tomoko greet us warmly outside their old farmhouse. Though we are the best of friends, we call him by his surname. So does his wife.

Ayako prepares a simple meal of tofu, fish and garden vegetables. As soon as it gets dark, we gather nets and glass jars and head outside. It's a remarkably clear night for *tsuyu.*

> stars, stars' reflections
> mirrored in the paddy field
> oh! the fireflies

They land on the grasses bordering the rice fields and on the *hotaru bukuro*, white bellflowers, that thrive in the damp soil. Tomoko plucks a bellflower for me and explains that *hotaru* means firefly and *bukuro* is sack. With our butterfly nets, we scoop the air and capture a net full of fireflies. Carefully we transfer them to the *hotaru bukuro* by opening the blossoms and inserting the fireflies into their petal-soft cage. Soon the flowers begin to take on the glow of the fireflies' light. By the end of an hour, we have a handful of lanterns to guide our way home. Other fireflies are contained in jars. How many do we have? Fifty? One hundred? It's impossible to count them with their lights flickering on and off, on and off.

At the farmhouse we remove our shoes and gather in the main room, settling down on the tatami. Murayama-san goes outside to his kiln and selects some sake cups from a recent firing. He presents each of us with a pristine cup and fills it with sake.

"*Kanpai!*" he toasts.

"*Kanpai!*" we echo, raising the smooth cups to our lips.

Our host closes all the *fusuma* doors to the rest of the house then opens the lids on the glass jars, releasing the fireflies into the room. Tomoko and I peel back the petals of the *hotaru bukuro* and coax our captives from their silken cages. They dart and flick, flash their green lights as they settle on arms and knees, and on the Japanese scroll in the alcove.

> lying on tatami
> in a room full of fireflies
> the evening cool

In the darkened room, we drink sake and talk softly, speak of gentle things, the importance of friendship, the natural abundance of life. For hours, we lie on the tatami whispering, as night deepens and the sake bottle empties. On the ceiling, the stars flicker on and off, on and off. When it's finally time to retire, Murayama-san opens the *shôji* and releases the fireflies into the night. By morning they will have scattered far and wide, specks of darkness against the overcast sky.

SUMMER

The rainy season stops in time for *Gion Matsuri*, the Kyôto festival that marks the beginning of summer. Thirty-one wooden floats called *hoko*, decorated with tapestries and ancient treasures, are pulled through the streets by men clad in loincloths and straw sandals. Those who are honored to be carried on the floats wear period costumes—wigs, multi-layered kimonos, and armor. They smile and wave, patiently enduring the heat. Thousands of people line the streets to watch the procession. There is a conviviality and magic that makes everyone forget *tsuyu* and the even hotter season to come.

University classes run till early July, making teaching a real challenge.

> teacher's question
> hangs in the drowsy classroom
> a crow answers

Even the farm women slow down.

> resting in the shade
> farm women gossip
> ripe tomatoes

Young people keep cool by going to horror movies and getting a chill up their spine. Older people prefer a traditional Noh ghost play.

old Noh actor
hands soft as a girl's
the quivering fan

closing his fan
the cool fragrance
of a kimono sleeve

John and I usually escape the hot Kyôto months, but the last summer, I remain alone in our house. At least I think I am alone.

Bewitched by *Tanuki*

Deep summer. I sit on the tatami with the *shôji* wide open in hopes of catching a cool breeze. Suddenly I'm startled by a movement from the garden. There, just six feet away, a furry animal stares back at me. We hold each others' eyes until, utterly fearless, he finally turns away.

Can this be a *tanuki*, the raccoon dog that Lafcadio Hearn writes about in his *Tales of the Mysterious*? Japanese translate *tanuki* as badger, but they look more like raccoons with their black masks and brown fur, except they are smaller and have longer legs. In Japanese folklore, the *tanuki* is a trickster. One of its favorite pranks is to transform itself into another animal—or even a human.

A few days later, I see him again. Though I've been thinking of it as a male, it is definitely female, a nursing mother with pink extended nipples. She comes closer this time; I move slowly towards her ready to close the *shôji* if she tries to enter the house. All I can think of are those sharp teeth that chewed up the leather sandals I left outside one night. But

Mama holds her ground, then turns and lumbers away. I throw out some fish scraps and am happy to see them gone in the morning. At dusk I hear a rustle in the garden and turn just in time to see a baby *tanuki* skitter across the moss. Then two others, like puppies, frolicking. One grabs my gardening glove and tears around with it, playing keep-away. I laugh out loud at their antics. Then they begin to scratch up the moss. They are adorable, but I have mixed feelings about them destroying our moss garden.

I am so excited that I call my friend, Michiko. "I have *tanuki* in my garden!"

"Impossible" she says. "Maybe you can find a *tanuki* in the countryside, but never in the city."

The next morning I am jolted awake by a squawk. Dressing quickly, I follow the sound to the abandoned house across the street. A baby *tanuki* has fallen into a deep hole. Mama and her two pups watch from a distance as I try to help. But the hole is too deep and narrow to go down and rescue him. I prop up a wooden plank into the hole hoping that with those sharp claws he'll be able to climb out.

> from a deep hole
> baby *tanuki* screeching
> ravens circle above

At dusk, the *tanuki* come once again to play in the garden and to eat the rice I've left out for them. I feel sad seeing only two babies instead of three. Mama crouches nearby and seems unconcerned. Do animals mourn the death of their off-spring?

The following evening is the annual fire festival at Tanuki-dani in the East Hills of Kyôto. To get to the Raccoon-Dog Temple, you must walk through a cedar forest, then climb more than a hundred stone steps to the top of the mountain. Although it's drizzling, I feel I should go there to say a prayer for the baby *tanuki* who died.

They are impressive, these old folks hiking up the stairs to receive the priest's blessing. Some have canes, others pull themselves up, step by step, holding onto the railing. Our ascent is punctuated by the beat of ancient drums played by *yamabushi*, wandering Shinto priests. Some of them carry a huge conch shell which they blow through to ward off evil. The sound is eerie, like a grieving animal.

At the top of the mountain, a crowd gathers around a bon-fire in the center of the courtyard. The *yamabushi* are dressed in robes with *tanuki* pelts fastened to a silk cord round their waists and hanging in the back, like a tail. Forming a circle, they chant sutras, joined by the old people who recite the religious texts from memory. Once the fire's burned down, priests from Tanuki-dani spread the embers with heavy wooden rakes. *Yamabushi* and Buddhist pilgrims, identified by their white robes, walk across first. Barefoot. I take my place at the end of the long line hoping that by the time my turn comes the coals will have been well tramped. When I walk across the coals, I am surprised that I feel no pain. On the contrary. Reaching the other side, I feel cleansed and renewed.

I take my time descending the stone steps back down the mountain. The sky has cleared and a full moon appears through gaps in the trees. The dim light from paper lanterns guides my way. I feel as though I'm under the *tanuki*'s spell.

The following evening, as usual, I throw chicken scraps out into the garden. And once again, the *tanuki* come—Mama and her pups. *Four* pups. Where did the fourth one come from? Not only did the third baby not die, but it seems to have reproduced itself.

> in my sandals
> the blessed ashes
> of Raccoon-Dog Temple

Autumn

One by one over the years, the ten houses on our lane have become vacant till John and I are the only ones living there.

> outside the empty hut
> a huddle of crickets
> their hollow voices

For Japanese, and for us too, autumn is a time of sadness,

watching the fish pond
fill up with shadows
   a distant train

lying side by side
separate letters
   from our divorced friends

but it is also a time for *momijigari*, maple viewing, at famous places such as Sanzen-in,

flying through gingkos	brown-robed monk
and then the maples	raking leaves into neat piles
how black the crow!	his new Adidas

and for bird watching.

> stalking the heron
> old man in a black beret
> aims his zoom lens

Farmers are busy with the rice harvest. For years, I have seen them cutting rice and have always wanted to join in. When I ask Lady B, she says, "Oh no, we have machines for that." But after a typhoon flattens the rice, I am allowed to help. I put on *kasuri* pants, a straw hat, and gloves and begin work. Japanese farm women stoop to cut the rice, but I'm so tall that I have to kneel.

> cutting the rice
> with quick hacks—
> the caterpillar so slow

I work with such focus that, when I finally look up, the farm women laugh at me from their circle where they are relaxing and drinking tea.

After the rice is cut, the sheaves are hung on bamboo poles to dry before they are taken down and threshed.

hanging the rice at dusk
the weary farmer
still wears his straw hat

dragonflies thrum
over the rice stubble
earthenware sunset

When the rice harvest is over, the cold season begins.

on the train
the smell of mothballs
early chill

wind blows
   the last brown leaves
clenched fingers

sun sets
behind bare trees
last persimmon

The last persimmon is always left on the tree for a traveler or for the birds.

WINTER

Winter in Kyôto is cold, especially in a traditional Japanese house. We spend many hours snuggled under the *kotatsu* drinking sake or green tea.

> long winter night
> tangerine peels
> piling up

The cold brings insects and animals inside. One night we hear a bang in the back hallway and spot a weasel foraging in the garbage. We chase him away, but in the middle of the night, we hear him knock the trash barrel over again. Weighting down the lid does no good; every morning there is garbage strewn in the hallway. Finally John buys some rope and secures the lid with a sailor's knot. The weasel can't open the trash bin. Neither can I.

I enjoy going on outings in winter because Japanese are sensitive to cold and the temples are always empty. My favorite temple in Ohara has a tatami room opened to the outdoors. Guests warm their hands over coals in the porcelain hibachi while old women in kimonos and white aprons serve us tea and rice cakes.

> hibachi embers—
> red berries
> dusted with snow

Winter is also a time for going within. Every January, I sit *zazen* at Sosen-ji, a Soto Zen temple. The evening begins with a lecture on Dôgen, followed by a one-hour sitting. Cold air seeping through the walls keeps me alert, but some meditators manage to doze off. The priest has a way of reviving those students.

hearing the whack	sunlight on tatami
of the Zen master's stick	the old Buddhist temple
my own shoulders twitch	smells of chrysanthemums

The year ends in a burst of activity. Everything must be cleaned—windows, cars, tatami—and *shôji* paper and *fusuma* replaced. They even have a name for it, *ôsôji,* end of the year cleaning. All unfinished business, such as paying debts, must be taken care of. Then there is the carving of *nenga-jo,* a woodblock print of the animal of the Chinese zodiac year. On top of everything, housewives spend days preparing special New Year's dishes so they won't have to cook over the holidays.

DARUMA

Every New Year's Eve we invite friends over to our house to celebrate. Like the Japanese, we eat a meal of *soba* noodles for long life and toast with sake drunk from small cups. Just before midnight, we bundle up and climb the hill to Yusen-ji, the oldest Nichiren sect temple. For twelve years, this has been our year-end tradition: to eat, drink, and ring the temple bell. On our last New Year's in Japan, however, something unusual happens.

When we arrive at the temple, people are already lined up around a bonfire. We have all come to ring the huge brass bell 108 times to rid the world of the 108 sins. As I wait in line, I remember last year's Daruma doll, which I have brought to burn. This doll is named after a Buddhist saint who vowed to sit in meditation until he became enlightened. He was so determined that he did not give up, even when his legs rotted off. Thus, Daruma symbolizes persistence and endurance. Made of papier maché, the dolls are round and have no legs. They are weighted so if they are knocked over, they right themselves. Daruma dolls come in all sizes. Mine was small, only four inches. In keeping with Japanese tradition, I bought it on the first day of the New Year, made a wish and drew in one of his eyes. Only when you have achieved your goal are you allowed to fill in the other eye.

I take the Daruma doll out of my pocket and toss it into the bonfire. It rolls out. All the Japanese go "E-EH-e-eee!" I pick it up and throw it back in. Out it comes again. By this time everyone is edging away from me. But I, too, am determined. I pick up my Daruma and throw it hard. This time it doesn't roll out.

> at year's end
> I burn the Daruma doll
> with only one eye

After ringing in the New Year, we walk to the Shinto shrine for the first sake, then home to sleep and dream the first dream of the year. A dream about Mt. Fuji brings you the most luck, a hawk second and lastly an eggplant.

We awaken feeling cleansed and refreshed. After breakfast we open the mailbox where *nenga-jo* are waiting. The post office holds these greeting cards, delivering bundles of them to each household on January 1.

hanging New Year's cards
on the *shôji*
last year's dust

New Year's Day is one of the few times of the year when Japanese dress in kimono as they visit the shrine to pay their respect and to buy amulets to keep them safe during the next year. The next few days are spent socializing with family and friends.

no footprints
outside the hermit's hut
on New Year's day

After the New Year celebrations, John and I begin to make preparations to leave Kyôto. We give away or sell most of our belongings. As the house empties, it becomes more fragile. The beams seem to lean more, the tatami look shabby, we notice that the latticed paper doors are out of kilter. All the nicks and discoloration in the walls stand out. The alcove looks forlorn with no flower arrangement or scroll. Without us and our belongings to keep it alive, the house has become the empty shell of a cicada.

leaving Japan
inside the paper lantern
a dusting of moths

end of summer
the rust on my scissors
smells of chrysanthemums

cushion, incense, bowl
so much preparation
to do nothing

Easter morning
the bread dough breathes and rises
under its damp cloth

late into the night
we talk of revelations
moon through the pines

silk sheets
gardenia on the bed stand
unfolds its petals

chickens no longer
dash to the compost
dregs of Chinese herbs

waking this morning
from troubled dreams
foxprints on new snow

spring wind
            raked stones in the dry garden
flow without moving

remembering those gone
thankful to be here—
pond of purple iris

Cid Corman

A Little Off the Track

As a fulltime poet—which means writing every day for over sixty years now—from the day I started (21 December 1941)—I thinkfeel in terms of every syllable and the spaces between words. (I never exaggerate.)

I often use the haiku syllabic structure but have never had any regard for haiku rules or any others. Every bit must work more than fully—immediately and constantly. If not, I have failed. And, as I have often said, anyone who can improve any poem of mine, by even a comma, is entitled to claim it as his or her own and with my blessing.

My earliest ambition was to be another and only Anon. And you will find most of my books (particularly those I designed and published) without my name on the title page or cover.

It's the poetry that matters, if it does, not my name.

And I have no idea when I find a poem in the offing—which could be at any moment—what it is going to singsay, let alone how. Each "form" is found, like each word, in the very making. Unstoppable. Immediate. Even in revisions over decades.

And the language for me must be simple (rare use of any adjectives)—everyday language. Even though very re-readable. Always more than you get at once.

A little off the track.

It isn't a matter of meaning, but of livingdying.

Of of.

15 November 2002
Utano

The Dawning

Whatever I say
a dewdrop says much better
saying nothing now.

Right O

We are the ones who
are no more than the ones we—
if that's the word—are.

We are going to—
there is no future in it—
is is the presence tense.

The stars are there not
to remind us but to let
us know what this is.

There is no end and
never was a beginning—so
here we are—amidst.

It's all been arranged
so you can forget it and
feel perfectly dead.

HELLO!

How do you do? How
do you? How—do—you—do—you?
You're asking too much.

Azaleas gone and
hydrangea trying to make
a show of it yet.

Alive or dead
I'm in it for
the poetry.

Everything
helps decipher
what nothing means.

Always that shudder
when the third eye winks
between the others.

Only a bunch of
swallows over and over
the darkening stream.

You are here—just as
I had imagined—
imagining me.

Nothing ends with you—
every leaf on the ground
remembering root.

Everything is
coming to a head—meaning:
blossoms yet to fall.

In the shadow of
the mountain the shadow of
any bird is lost.

I wear the mask of
myself and very nearly
get away with it.

How to learn to be
ignorant? Any scholar
provides an example.

Your shadow
on the page
the poem.

In the river skeins
of sunlight and sky fastened
to the moment's dye.

You'll never get to
the end of me—I doubt if
I'll get there either.

In the mirror for
a moment it almost all
seems possible.

The Counsel

Live with the living
die with the dying
and there you are: here.

Nothing says it all—
which is just why I'm trying
to tell you nothing.

Existence

All you have
and all you
have to give.

Diane di Prima

About Haiku

At first it was a crossroads, the non-existent spot where time and space crossed each other at right angles. Later, both time and space (in the sense of dimensionality) disappeared and there was timelessness (not even the "event out of time" as H.D. has it). Something infinitesmal and particular. Most recently it's been all about spaciousness, vastness in the fewest possible strokes. Images. Letting the breath open the sky.

the inner tide—
what moon does it follow?
I wait for a poem

too much wind
the poppies
refuse to open

for days that old dream
like a window on an unimagined landscape
& the sun about to rise

Death Poems In April

I

even the Buddha lay down
to breathe his last.
why am I struggling?

2

easy to disappear
into this fog

3

pour this water and ash
on the roots
of some old tree

DREAM POEM ON THE CALIFORNIA INDIANS
(after reading Kroeber)

song cycles
lost in the woods:
the last throat pierced

ANCIENT HISTORY

the women are lying down
in front of the bulldozers
sent to destroy the last of the olive groves

INDEPENDENCE DAY 2002

bald eagle
making a come-back
so am I

Three "Dharma Poems"

1

his vision or not?
gone is the authority
w/ which he opened his fan.

2

raindrops melt in the pond
& it's hard to say
just what "lineage" is

3

my faith—
what is it but ancient dreams
of wild ones in the mountains?

FROM HARBIN HOT SPRINGS
(In a season of drought)

1

in the gray light
jays scream
at departing guests

2

spring mist, scant green
on these ancient hills
the ground still parched

3

no February mushrooms
at the foot of the bay tree
the deer chews old roots

The Widow's Smile

a ten haiku sequence

I

the widow's smile
as she arranges winter roses
in a glass

2

marks of the
jackrabbit's teeth on every
pad of the prickly pear

3

laughter of the thin child
on her way
to cancer surgery

4

old man's mind
flares brightly as he
writes the last page of his journal

5

even off-season
the cholla
flowers

6

died in yr sleep
laid out in yr own bed:
how did the dream change?

7

cold winter morning
the baby quail search for seeds
under the sagebrush

8

dawn over mountains
in the dead tree
the ladder-back woodpecker is ready

9

would like to hold you
in silence, say yes
grief is as you describe it

10

in the dry wash
tracks of coyote
white bones of something small

last night it rained
here and there pumpkins
gleam in white fog

do they tremble from
wind, from noise, or pleasure:
green plants at an open window

SHORT POEMS ON THE AFGHAN WAR

1

small bones of
mountain children
in the snow

2

bags of rice burst open
burlap flaps in the wind
even the label "USA" is fading

3

WE AIR-DROP TRANSISTOR RADIOS

can you eat them?
will they
keep you warm?

AFTER GENJI

In the dream we didn't even seek to touch.
How susceptible the heart in the morning
rain!

Patricia Donegan

An Antidote to Speed

clear water is cool
fireflies vanish——
there's nothing more
—Chiyo-ni, 1703-1775

Japanese haiku, the simple three-line form of poetry, is now the world's most popular poetic form. Since it first became known in the West one hundred years ago, it has been seen from various perspectives. As a way to convey an aesthetic image, as a way to appreciate nature and as a way to record the Zen ah! moment. Perhaps it could also be seen as a means to appreciate "transience"—a way (or perhaps a practice) to enable us to understand and accept death in our ourselves and everything around us.

Haiku brings us the birth and death of each moment. Everything is stripped away to its naked state. No high tech speed, but slowly and naturally we discover what is simply here, as in meditation: our aging bodies, the afternoon light on the bed sheets, the sound of a siren in the distance. Whatever is contained in this very moment, without adornment. The *Tibetan Book of the Dead* talks about these momentary *bardo* states, states of transition from one realm to another, from life to death to re-birth. These states of transition also exist in each moment of our life when we are alive on this earth, each moment containing a mini-birth and mini-death. One result of America's shock of September 11, 2001 was a greater recognition of this transience, on an individual, national and world level of consciousness.

Usually it takes a personal crisis such as a death or separation from a loved one to awaken this realization of our true human condition. It is really our inability to accept this impermanence that causes us to appreciate less and suffer more. As Pema Chodron, a Tibetan meditation teacher says,

> "… happiness lies in being able to relax with our true condition which is basically fleeting, dynamic, fluid, not in any way solid, not in any way permanent. It's transient by nature …"

> violets, grow here and there
> in the ruins
> of my burned house
> —Shokyu-ni, 1713-1781

However, in the midst of the speed of postmodern culture, we somehow miss this point. The effect of speed is that it ignores, denies or negates the natural process of life. For things take time to grow: a garden, a baby's steps, the trust of a friend, the study of a map or the stars, even a good cup of coffee or tea. This was recently illustrated in a Japanese comic strip showing the making of a cup of Japanese tea: a hundred years ago, one hour to make and serve tea in tea-ceremony style; fifty years ago, fifteen to thirty minutes to boil water in a kettle and serve tea in a ceramic cup; twenty years ago, five minutes to steep a tea-bag from a hot-pot into a paper cup; ten years ago, five seconds to get a hot can of tea from a vending machine (See *Kyôto Journal* #47, p. 91). Modern civilization's evolution or "de-evolution"?

A speedy culture ignores natural laws. For through this unconscious addiction to speed and hyper-living, even in the simple act of drinking a cup of tea, the natural process of birth, growth, old age and death is given little attention. No part of this is escaped, but the process is missed. Any transformation emerging from reflection is bypassed. And without self-reflection, especially reflection of our mortality, we cannot really see ourselves or our world clearly. This is where haiku awareness can possibly bridge the gap—as a practice to be more conscious of these momentary states in our lives.

> plucking my gray hairs—
> beside my pillow
> a cricket sounds
>
> —Bashô, 1644-1694

Haiku can be an antidote to the speed of post-modern culture, allowing one to step off the spinning wheel, to stop and breathe deeply and slowly. To note the birth and death of each moment. Whether we write it down, recording it in words, isn't of ultimate importance, although it may be enjoyable for some. But rather, seeing things around us with "haiku eyes" is of importance,

Haiku awareness can be a vehicle to help bring our attention back to the moment. Reading good traditional or modern haiku can give us a hint as to how to be more present. Haiku's brevity, too, fits the short attention span of a speedy world. In fact, the process of tracing the rising and falling of this moment's birth and death is built into this three-line Japanese poetic form, which makes it one of the easiest art forms to use in expanding this kind of awareness.

> rising steam from the bath—
> spring begins
> on this moonlit night
>
> —Issa, 1762-1826

Expanding awareness means noticing what is already here in this time and space. Noticing for a few moments, perhaps only for as long as the count of 1, 2 or 3 breaths ... Letting the thoughts and sensations of the moment's sounds and images fade and new sensations arise. Perhaps noting the fading sunlight on the curtain ... That moment dies and another is born; no need to catch it but just note its passing, as a thought in meditation, as in a last breath, as in the loss of something which becomes dearer because it's fleeting.

This traditional Japanese life view, an acceptance of *mujo* or transience, is naturally embedded in haiku. This aesthetic in Japanese is known as *mono no aware*, which roughly translates as "the beauty of dying things" or "the beauty of transient things." Rather than a traditional Western poetry of denial in "rage, rage against the dying of the light" (Dylan Thomas) or "Death, thou shalt die" (John Donne), Japanese traditional poetry shows an acceptance and awe of the natural stages of becoming and disappearing in each thing. As in these haiku:

> summer grasses—
> the only remains
> of warriors' dreams
>
> —Bashô

> good-bye
> I pass like all things
> dew on the grass
>
> —Banzan, 1661-1730

the dead body—
autumn wind blows
through its nostrils

—Iida Dakotsu, 1885-1962

And although it's possible to find the opposite view in each tradition, nonetheless, these two views of acceptance and denial still pervade the cultures of the "East and West."

Whether we ultimately accept or deny, the main thing is to note the passing of things. That in itself is transformative, as it forces us to slow down. For in the speed of modern culture, instead of using "saved time" to be quiet, sit still and just be, as in slower, less "high tech" cultures, we instead do another thing—go to another appointment, travel a further distance, and wonder why we have "less time." Our modern litany is, "I don't have enough time." Speed accelerates, draws us into the vortex, so instead of doing less we are doing more.

The speed of Western-style globalized culture has a dehumanizing effect. It ironically defeats our original purpose: to have more time to relax and enjoy the moment. Haiku may be a way to step out of this vortex, if only for a few moments a day. To write it down, or just stop and note the moment's passing will inevitably force us to slow our pace, so that we can participate in the moment's birth and death. It is essential for our survival, for even our health and sanity, but above all for our humanness.

I kill an ant
realize my children
have been watching

—Hekigodo

As I look up from writing down these thoughts about "haiku and transience" in Zenpukuji Park near my house in Tokyo, the autumn day turns to dusk. I note the pale gray light descending and shimmering in waves across the surface of the pond; the wild ducks floating in the dimming light. I note the stillness and the passing of the light in the ending of the day; the shouts of nearby children squealing with delight. The scene makes me wonder ... the ducks or clouds don't seem to be moving any faster than they did when I was a kid, or I imagine even a hundred years ago, but it is us human beings who are moving faster than is natural.

We are losing something vital, and we know it; we can feel it, an unbearable emptiness from loss. Empty because we are disconnecting from the slower rhythm of life around us, away from the slower pace of each moment's passing. This disconnection seems to create a deep, unspeakable loneliness within us. And as we connect more and more to the instant-electronic net, we seem further and further disconnected from the natural net, the web of life. Ironically, in other eras when human beings were more connected to natural rhythms, they wrote haiku but didn't need to use it in the way we do today.

To relax with our true human condition which is itself

transient, we must slow down enough to be aware, to feel the gap, the crack in the universe's egg. For without seeing what is here, we are just speeding past and seeing very little. It reminds me of taking the *Shinkansen* (bullet train) from Tokyo to Kyôto: it saves time, about three hours, but you see a blur instead of relaxing scenery; and in fact, one gets a headache if one stares out the window to see a view at all. We need to slow down, even for a few minutes, with whatever is in our sphere.

Breathing in and out with the ducks across the pond, breathing in and out with the rising and falling of the red maple branches, breathing in and out with the sick spouse or child sleeping next to us, just noting that ... This is our heritage as human beings with all the other sentient beings on our planet. And haiku awareness in this post-modern era can be a vehicle leading us not back to another slower time, which is virtually impossible, but back to this very moment, if just for a moment.

> the first mists—
> one mountain after another
> unveiled
> —Chiyo-ni

pampas grass
bending—
endless dreams

following the silence
to the open field—
the galaxies

last night lightning
this morning
the white iris

long walk—
cherry petals stick
to the bottoms of my shoes

summer twilight—
a woman's song
mingles with the bath water

winter afternoon
not one branch moves—
I listen to my bones

first moonlight
fills
the trumpet flower

maple leaves
barely moving
in the earthquake

halfway
up the mountain—
the silence

moon-lit night:
a bone
is broken

pampas grass bends
bodies
intertwined

still
spring night—
a gunshot

frosty moon—
the shoes
you left

rising sun
over the blue mountains—
cremation smoke

as raindrops diminish
I hear the tapping
of the monk's wooden bell

after the bombing
the trace
of a moon

over Nagasaki
on a clear night
the Milky Way

in between
the Kabul bombings
voices of crickets

a dragonfly
peeks into
the empty torpedo

in-between
the howling wind
the pouring of sake

noon heat—
the cockroach naps
under the kitchen table

one red maple leaf
in the drain
of the shower

spring
crowds of people
one, two a Buddha

spring wind—
I too
am dust

PENNY HARTER

Seeing and Connecting

I have been writing haiku for thirty years and longer poems for almost forty. Writing haiku opens my mind, my senses, and my spirit. It helps me get in touch with what is most important—paying attention to what I've called, "that click in the gut," or "leap of the spirit." When asked to define poetry, I have always said that writing a poem is, first and foremost, an act of seeing, followed by connecting. Writing haiku helps me to feel a relationship between myself and other, so that, in a way, I become other.

While some writers believe that haiku must only be written from immediate and actual experience, others create haiku from long ago memory, from fantasy, or from combining the real and the imaginary. I believe that both immediate experiences and remembered or imaginative perceptions are valid haiku sources. For me, haiku must be brief and image-centered, and devoid of overt metaphor or simile. Both my haiku and longer poems result from a sudden awareness of connection between a perception and the feelings that arise from it, or from my sensing a unique relationship between and among aspects of the object or experience perceived, remembered, or created.

Haiku should show what the poet experienced that made him or her have a certain response, and if the poet has done a good job, the reader has a similar response when reading the haiku.

Although most haiku seem to center on moments in nature, others need not do so; instead, verses may comment on human interactions with the natural world or with one another, and on human activities and observances. For example, after a particularly difficult discussion with my then thirteen-year-old daughter, I wrote:

closed bedroom door—
her shadow darkens
the crack of light

Another time I experienced a synthesis that made me wonder about the use of the heavens for warfare, or just cluttering them with tons of space junk:

distant thunder
overhead a satellite
moves in the dark

I believe it is important to set the poem in a particular time and place, to use present tense for immediacy, and to keep it short (one to three lines). I have even written a few one-line haiku, inviting the reader to experiment with the location of the break or "turn" so characteristic of the best haiku:

mallards leaving in the water rippled sky

I could have divided this poem in several places, but to do so would have disturbed the unbroken gliding of the ducks from the water into the sky. I wanted the reader to feel all the possibilities, such as "mallards leaving—/ in the water / rippled sky" or "mallards / leaving in the water / rippled sky." Haiku can certainly teach us the importance of appropriate line breaks, and I have applied what I learned about line-breaking in haiku to my longer poems. Also, I avoid rhyme since overbearing sound can detract from the image.

Haiku can also be connected to create a sequence, moving from moment to moment of the perceived experience. On a trip to Japan in 1997, I wrote the following. As I read it now, I revisit the time and place:

The Scent of Cedar

At Nikko Toshogu Shrine, for Yatsuka Ishihara

stone lantern—
five chambers rise
in the cedar's shade

broken cedar stump
its mildewed center open
to the Earth

mist between the cedars
and on the far hillside
a forest of mist

on the cedar slope
cut pieces of a trunk
touch each other

stone lanterns
darken in the dusk—
the scent of cedar

During the summer of 1987 my husband and I were for-
tunate enough to spend the night in a pilgrims' dormitory on
Mount Haguro in Yamagata Prefecture, Japan. When I
entered the room, its entire far end open to the sky, I quickly

crossed the space to the edge of the tatami-matted floor and opened my arms:

> fingertip to fingertip
> and still more sky—
> Mount Haguro

That is how haiku happen. For me, each haiku I write is like breathing out, giving back to the earth recognition, affirmation, and gratitude. I am reminded of how seldom we really notice what is going on around us, and how important the most ordinary things can be. Writing haiku is one way of translating the Earth—honoring what the mountain, the dragonfly, the neighbor, and even the dirt under our feet mean to our existence. Whether we know it or not, we are one with them. The writing and sharing of haiku can bring us together as we celebrate our connections with the larger world that we share, while at the same time affirming the particular times and places of our lives and our human responses to them.

> beekeeper
> humming
> back

full moon—
light in the cracks
of the sidewalk

missing the bus
the old man hugs
the bus-stop sign

distant thunder—
overhead, a satellite
moves in the dark

nightfall—
the coolness of dirt
between toes

closed bedroom door—
her shadow darkens
the crack of light

all night
the sound of your breathing
the autumn wind

in the graveyard
the mourners slap
at mosquitoes

before sleep
he opens the window
to let in the rain

moonlight gleaming
on the grapes—the lovers
can't stop laughing

snowmelt—
on the banks of the torrent
small flowers

following the guide-rail
the blind man
gets a splinter

the homeless man
takes off his shoes before
his cardboard house

autumn wind—
in the clear broth
the taste of seaweed

measuring the fencepost,
the inchworm stops, leans out
into space

without looking
the butcher cleaves the shoulder
between the bones

through the telescope
the mountains on the moon—
grandmother yawns

evening rain
I braid my hair
into the dark

through the empty
wine glass on the sill—
the moonlit sea

looking through the telescope
the child asks
What time is it?

before her wedding
I zip my daughter's dress
so slowly

down from the mountain
the same cicada
the same rock

New Year's Eve—
I feed my birthday cards
to the fire

TV off
the screen reflects
a living room

days end—
the fortuneteller
takes off her glasses

CHRISTOPHER HEROLD

Episodes

Over the past twenty-five years or so, my own understanding and practice of haiku have undergone many changes and refinements. I've learned countless valuable lessons from fellow haiku poets. Even so, I find it difficult to find words that adequately describe the overall effect this miraculous form of expression has had in shaping my life. As an alternative, I'd like to share two episodes that illustrate basic states of mind that, to me, seem essential for appreciating haiku moments. Neither episode involves haiku directly but both nudged me towards the awareness from which haiku naturally arise. Each involved a teacher. Both were Japanese. Neither was a haiku poet.

EPISODE ONE

The year was 1968. I was twenty years old and the youngest student attending a training session at Tassajara, the first Soto Sect, Zen Buddhist monastery to be established in the United States. The grueling five-day initiatory period was finally over and new students were assigned various jobs. Mine was to dig rocks out of a large plot of ground destined to become the monastery vegetable garden. It was next to that rocky field that the first teaching took place.

A few days earlier, I'd unwittingly penned my first "haiku," at least that's what the head monk told me it was. To me, what I'd written was simply a verbal response to a heightened state of consciousness. The subsequent lesson didn't have to do with my poem and my teacher had no intention of instructing me on some essential aspect of wordcraft. What I learned had to do with paying close attention.

The teacher was Shunryu Suzuki, *Roshi*, the founding Abbot of San Francisco Zen Center and Tassajara. He was also an avid gardener. Even during the last few years of his life, as his health was failing, Suzuki could be found pruning, weeding, or even wrestling large stones into place by his cabin.

My job didn't require a gardener's aesthetic know-how. Removing rocks from the soil is just hard work, but I was expected to apply myself to the task whole-heartedly, with attention fully focused. *Roshi* (which means "venerable old teacher" and is how everyone addressed Suzuki) would occasionally walk past while I was sweating away with a pick or shovel. He'd always smile and nod. As brief as those gestures were, he was completely present in them. I sensed his appreciation and immediately felt invigorated. Once, I was so grateful for *Roshi's* spirit-boosting smile that I wanted to give him something, anything. Looking down, I spotted a shiny green acorn, still snug in its brown cap. There were thousands lying around but I picked that one, trotted over to Suzuki, bowed, and handed it over. He gazed at it for what seemed to me a couple of minutes. Twenty seconds was probably more like it. We both studied the acorn intently. What at first I took to be a common nut began to reveal distinct characteristics. Every detail stood out as though viewed under a magnifying glass—slender striations in the smooth green surface, the regular pattern of scales on the cap, a small brown streak along one curve. I became acutely aware of the acorn's potential: the tree within it.

Suzuki carefully put the acorn in a pocket inside his robe. We then bowed to each other and he walked away. I went back to digging. No words were spoken, nevertheless a dialogue took place. What was communicated is still with me today. I was just one of many students at Tassajara, one acorn among many. I was also unique and special. In the same way, haiku are at their best when the words are transcended and we go directly to the extraordinary nature of ordinary things. In order to better appreciate what we find in this world we must take the time to pay close attention.

Twenty-five years and several occupations later, my Tassajara lesson was reinforced from a different perspective. The year was 1993, my new teacher was a Japanese nurseryman. I had begun a small business as a landscaper and gardener. One afternoon, I was painstakingly picking through a stack of flagstones at a local nursery, trying to find just the right sizes and shapes for a project. The nurseryman strolled over to watch me make my selections. After a while he asked how I was planning to use the stones. I told him they were for a path I was building from a client's front garden to the tea house in her back yard. He considered this for a moment, then shook his head. "A garden path should never do that," he said. "It shouldn't lead from here to there. It should lead from here to here, to slow people down so they can appreciate what is right here, right now."

I'm fairly certain that the nurseryman misread the expression on my face. To him, my blank look probably meant that I hadn't understood what he'd said. I did understand him, however, and very much appreciated what he had to say. What startled me was the tantalizing notion that I'd come face to face with the reincarnation of haiku master, Bashô. As the story goes, Bashô's Zen teacher was perturbed by his student's devotion to haiku. He felt poetry to be a distraction from meditation practice. One day the teacher (Butcho) asked Bashô to tell him what was so special about haiku. Bashô responded that it is "simply what is happening in this place at this moment." Butcho was deeply impressed, and so was I when the nurseryman made his comment. It was then I realized that, although I'd practiced meditation and haiku for years, and had read untold numbers of books on those subjects, I still wasn't living my life in accordance with what I knew. The nurseryman's brief lesson was yet another wake up call.

It's an interesting coincidence that both of these lessons took place in the context of garden work—the first while I was involved with removing stones, the second while I was in involved with placing them.

Both the nurseryman and Shunryu Suzuki helped teach me that, to appreciate a garden, a haiku, or anything else in life, it is important to ease my grip on goals, to slow down and take notice. I placed those stepping stones so that they not only led from one place to another but from here to here. Seven years later, I arranged the haiku in my book, *A Path in the Garden,* with the same intention. Each haiku is an invitation to pause and to take a look around. For me, haiku is more than a form of written expression; it's a practice that helps me to wake up and live more abundantly.

a touch
the sea anemone
swallows itself

a warm gust ...
back through the gate it comes
the whole pile of leaves

nearing the roses
    a swallowtail
        from glide to flutter

gate unlatched
to and fro a lizard rides
the creaking breeze

hot night—
within the din of crickets
a single cricket

elevator silence
our eyes escape
into numbers

dark, dark night
a leaf strikes the pavement
stem first

bird shadow
    from tree shadow
        to fence shadow

open window
a mockingbird song
the length of twilight

just a minnow
the granite mountain wobbles
on the lake

first light
everything in this room
was already here

overcast morning
a few seeds still dangle
from the dandelion

moonrise . . .
screams from the roller coaster
no longer seem near

weathered wooden walk
grains of sand blown in, blown out
of a knothole

almost dawn
cupped in the curve of the moon
the rest of the moon

foghorns
we lower a kayak
into the sound

a breeze ...
again the neighbor's windchimes
belong to me

beach of pebbles
the chosen one skips
into a new year

scissor-snip
pollen sprinkles the back
of one hand

a ray of sun
pierces the lowering clouds
the heron leans forward

autumn sunset
the wake of a tugboat
sloshes ashore

Independence Day
　　　reservation Indians
　　　selling fireworks

cherry tree
without blossoms, without leaves,
moonlight

not quite dawn
someone stops trying
to start a car

river's end . . .
the sound of my name in the hiss
of receding surf

moth consumed
        the candle flame again
                unwavering

first light
a butterfly dries its wings
under wild blue sky

WILLIAM J. HIGGINSON

Santa Fe Shopping Carts

—for Paul Conneally

The brand-new store comes with brand-new shopping carts, and in the first few weeks when there is lots of help around and people are impressed with the new carts, there are few casualties. However, as the first month or so passes, one or another suffers a bent caster housing and a wheel that has its own direction in mind. Other carts develop flat-sided wheels; pushing one of them is like moving crosswise over a dirt road. Finally, a wheel breaks off altogether, leaving a gleaming axle that soon picks up stray mop strands.

Such carts gradually congregate—usually at the back of the in-store cart corral. Near the end of a long day they are often the only carts left in the store, the personnel situation having deteriorated along with the condition of the carts. A few stragglers, hardier than their shut-in cohorts, staunchly defend their rights to various choice car-parking spaces. They're not about to move on without a lot of coaxing.

The occasional cart, borrowed temporarily to wheel the groceries to a tract-house, ends up in a nearby arroyo, where its baby seat becomes the base for a birds-nest. When the monsoon season hits, mid-summer, the cart sinks into the silt and catches debris, thus ensuring its permanent place in the landscape.

> summer storm . . .
> a shopping cart rolls past
> the end of the lot

Sometimes a cart is trundled off in its prime by a human who employs it to carry all worldly possessions. Such a cart may be seen shining through the dusty leaves of a small grove of Russian olive trees, or gleaming dully where the river has gone dry in the shade under a bridge.

> socks hang . . .
> air crisp through the chrome
> of the shopping cart

Even this lucky cart, however, serves only its allotted time. Come winter, the homeless person sleeps in the library during the day, keeping on the move at night, or possibly signing in at a shelter for a night out of the gritty wind.

By early spring, it is time for a shipment of new shopping carts.

> deep in the arroyo
> just the red handle
> of a shopping cart

Holding the water,
  held by it—
    the dark mud.

This Alamo:
    too small a place
      for dying.

neglected roses
among the blasted
buds one
perfect white

hard fall

slowly
checking
the un-
sheathed
      axe

before the descent
musing then seeing
the sudden bluebird

Segovia: Bach
and the scent of insects
burnt in the lamp

the train tracks
bumpier
second day on the bike

municipal court—
a lawyer passes his colleague
the funny papers

the city boy
is the only one listening—
the song of the frogs

death dream . . .
I struggle awake to the cry
of a mourning dove

a white dog
sinks its muzzle to sniff
deep in the snow

a gun in the wildflowers
one young man
more or less

the withered iris
leans on the fresh
immaculate bloom

how could the cat know?
this dead fledgling too
was someone's child

—for Rujana Matuka

that cicada after
so long so shrill, flew
silver in twilight

—for Shinkû Fukuda

cherry-petal shells ...
even the sand-crabs live
in that light

in the depths
of the cat's eyes—
spring darkness

the raven's wings
floating on the wind—
sky mirror

—*for Sachiyo Itô*

moonlight glitters—
    the edge of a spread fan
        slices smoke

Elizabeth Searle Lamb

Illuminations

Haiku is to capture the moment: light on a bricked-up window in Greenwich Village, faint crowing of a rooster early in the morning after a death has come, colored sails in an Amazon harbor after rain. It is to track down the elusive dream: a white raven in the desert, an abandoned water tower, the real wetness of incomprehensible tears. It is to resurrect a tiny prism of memory into a moment that lives with color, scent, sound. These are, for me, the functions of haiku, senryu, and the short lyric. Captured in the amber of words, the moment endures.

spring morning
a green gate opens into
the apple orchard

pausing
halfway up the stair—
white chrysanthemums

taking a deep breath ...
a grove of jack pines,
unlogged

the sound
of rain on the sound
of waves

silence—
the heart of the rose
after the wasp leaves

a raven
that dark gutteral sound
his shadow

a single shoe
in the median
rush hour

the first August rain
suddenly a double rainbow
that stays   and stays

by the hollyhocks
suddenly
I straighten up

tossing a stone
down an old mine shaft—
the setting sun

sure of the news
even before I answer the phone
how cold my hands are

she waits
for the bee in her hair
to disengage

before tonight's frost
bringing in a cricket's song
with the geraniums

shutting out the cold
but grief still enters
by another door

one red leaf
falls from a poinsettia—
the harpist tuning

the sweet bite
of homemade sake   spring sleet
against the window

the year turns—
on the harp's gold leaf
summer's dust

the first fall of snow
even quieter, inside
the small adobe

New Year's Eve
all the whistles, all the bells
but in the fog   ghosts

the crunch of snow
under this cold blue moon
bells of the New Year

my shadow
I follow it all the way
home

the old album:
not recognizing at first
my own young face

dust from the ore tailings
a flash of tanager wings
in the hot sun

so heavily
the two buzzards lift
from the deer carcass

such small sounds ...
the silence of the night
deepens

wings of the wild geese,
their shadows trailing behind ...
the iced-in lake

tiny winged creature
no less beautiful
without a name

MICHAEL MCCLURE

Haiku Edge

Classic haiku originate in Japan's seasons and special subjects. "Haiku Edge" comes from where I live in the hills near the San Francisco Bay, where deer cross the street from a patch of forest to chew on fallen plums and great horned owls court in the darkness, and where there are bandaids stuck to the streets and etched in moonlight.

This world of "Haiku Edge" has its own seasons: the rainy season when waterfalls gurgle, and the dry summer when chain saws screech. Helicopters fly over the glens and streets at any time.

Beat poet and retired Buddhist monk, Zenshin Ryufu Philip Whalen, explained to me, in the 1950s, how a haiku should be written in English. He showed me the ellipsis, the mirroring or the reflection of the two parts of the poem's action. (Much like what happens in the longer tanka.)

The haiku opens what Mahayana Buddhists call "realms." Everything dissolves into the perception that initiates the poem.

Some haiku are soft and make the originating perception snug. *Wabi* (countrified gnarliness) and the clear light of elegance may come together in haiku. There are also harsh haiku.

Samuel Butler said, in effect, that life is a violin solo but you are learning to play the violin in public as you go. Like a violin sonata, haiku must have many rules to give freedom to the imagination.

"Raphael found the rules and was freed." The rules became clear as I wrote "Haiku Edge." First I abandoned seventeen syllables, which is over-ample in English.

The lines of capital letters in "Haiku Edge" are not meant to be emphasized. Read "Haiku Edge" aloud, and the poems can be seen as energy constructs and the eccentricities of typography will disappear.

In public performance at music clubs and colleges Ray Manzarek accompanies my reading of haiku on piano. Manzarek says he's "playing the words." We make a scroll of voice and music to float the poems, like parchment or silk supporting *sumi* ink.

OH ACCIDENT!
Oh,
per
fect
((CRUSHED))
snail
—LIKE
A
STAR
gone out
!

HEY, IT'S ALL CON
SCIOUSNESS
—thumps
of assault
rifles
and
the
stars

WHAT SOFT
brown eyes
the dog has
as
she
shits
on the deer's
hoof
print

THE DUSTY
blackberry
shakes
in
the
CHOP
PER
ROAR
—AH
the spider
web
!

DROPS
OF RAIN
((MIR
ROR))
on the pink
petals
of
the
peyote
flower

THE BIG
YELLOW
LEAF
S
P
I
N
S
through
the silver
down
pour.
—Smacks
my

wind
shield

PINK BANDAID STUCK
to the asphalt
looks gray
in
moon
light

while
crick
ets
sing

MOLDY
BOARD
SMELL
!
((AH))
MY
Grand
pa's
face
appears
in
the air

for Norma

NOTH
ING
NESS
of
intelligence;
silver
sunlight
through
closed
eyelids

OH
HUM
MING
BIRD
SHAD
OW
on the black
plum
!
((No summer lightning
though))

freeway

FOUR DEER
and
a great
blue
heron
in a field.
Brake
lights
up
a
head
!

for Allen Ginsberg

MAROON
suitcase
by
a
garbage can.
My
white
breath
in
air

the mystery

IT'S SKINNY
like

a

cooper hawk

and flies

through

fog

and

car

roars

WIND blows WAVES
on brown
puddles
and makes
black
clouds
like
breathing

PLUM
petals
fall when
the
old
dog's
nails
click
on
the
asphalt

for James Broughton

THE DRY
fir needle
rolling
in
the wind
has
a
shad
ow

MONKEY
fingered,
PINE
BOUGH
TIPS
reach

up

in

silver
fog

THE FOX TURD
is a cliff
a
n
d
the
butterfly
is
a
condor

SPARKLY FLIES
crawl through
the dead mole's
black fur
in sun
light

THE TINY GREEN-BLACK SNAKE
makes no dust cloud
as he speeds away

summer hummingbird

A
SCARLET HEAD
and long beak
float
in
mist
and
leaves.
THIS
NECTAR
HUNT
!

for Harry

THE
MILKY
WAY
IS
another
shiny
cricket
chirping
while leaves
fall

TREES
MOVING IN THE WIND
WERE
ONCE
protons
or
imagination

MMM,
TASTE
OF
DUST
on
the tongue
just
as
the crow
caws

UNDER THE FUR
the skin's
like
butter,
the purr
is
a
roar

for Bruce Conner

BUTTERFLIES
swirling madly.
Ah,
light shows
at the Avalon!

P
I
N
E
C
O
N
E
and candle
burn
at opposite
ends
of zazen

for Robin and Richard

THE WILD
IRIS
TREM
bles

in
the

plane roar,
yellow violet.

for Jack and Adelle

RAIN MIRROR
for
the
sky
and an old dog
stumbles by

Sonia Sanchez

The Haiku For Me Is

Silence. crystals. cornbread
and greens laughter. brocades.
The sea. Beethoven. Coltrane.
Spring and winter. blue rivers.
Dreadlocks. blues. a waterfall.
Empty mountains. bamboo. bodegas.
Ancient generals. dreams. lamps.
Sarah Vaughn. Her voice exploding
in the universe, returning to earth
in prayer. Plum blossoms.
Silk and steel. Cante jondo.
Wine. hills. flesh. perfume.
A breath inhaled and held.
Silence.

1
Come windless invader
I am a carnival of
Stars a poem of blood.

2
I have caught fire from
Your mouth now you want me to
Swallow the ocean.

3
When we say good-bye
I want yo tongue inside my
Mouth dancing hello.

4

Mixed with day and sun
I crouched in the earth carry
You like a dark river.

5

You too slippery
For me. Can't hold you long or
Hard. Not enough nites.

6

Am I yo philly
Outpost? Man when you sail in
To my house, you docked.

7

This is not a fire
Sale but I am in heat
Each time I see ya.

8

I am who I am.
Nothing hidden just black silk
Above two knees.

9

I am you loving
My own shadow watching
This noontime butterfly.

10
Is there a fo rent
Sign on my butt? You got no
Territorial rights here.

11
My face is a scarred
Reminder of your easy
Comings and goings.

12
Derelict with eyes
I settle in a quiet
Carnival of waves.

13
I want to make you
Roar with laughter as I ride
You into morning.

14
I have carved your face
On my tongue and I speak you
In my off-key voice.

15
the I in you the
you in me colliding in
one drop of semen

16
legs wrapped around you
camera. Action. Tightshot.
This is not a rerun.

17
Sonku

What I want
From you can
You give me? What
I give to
You do you
Want? Hey? Hey?

18

love between us is
speech and breath. Loving you is
a long river running.

STEVE SANFIELD

Only the Ashes

In the fall of 1980 I was in Jonesborough, Tennessee at the National Storytelling Festival. I was planning to drive from there to northern Kentucky to visit friends. It was early afternoon, and before leaving I stopped at a roadside cafe to get a bite for the road. Seated in the booth across from me was a Japanese woman whom I guessed to be in her mid-thirties. There are not many Japanese in that part of the country, but what intrigued me even more was that she was intently writing in a notebook. I approached and asked if I might join her. Fortunately she spoke much more English than I did Japanese.

Before we finished our meal, I learned she was passing through. "Just seeing some of your country," as she put it. Our conversation became more personal, and what ultimately drew us together was the discovery that we were both longing for a lost love.

That evening, at a local motel, she introduced me to these poems. She told me she'd found them in a partially-filled notebook in a secondhand store in Osaka. The poems were written in an elegant script but were unsigned. The notebook was dated 1928.

For two days and two nights we worked together on English versions of the poems. I began to suspect they were actually her own, but before I could ask her directly she was gone. When I woke on that third morning there was a bundle of thirty-one poems (we had worked on many more) and a note that said: *These are yours now. Thank you.*

It was signed *Kage*, just *Kage*, which I've since learned means "shadow."

> How many days now?
> The calendar says six.
> The heart has lost count.

Obsessed with the thought
that our shadows
will never mingle again.

Now that he's gone
I even crave
the endless waiting.

His last words to me
were words of love.
They only bind me tighter.

Is there anything
I could have done
to keep him here?

Why bother to brush my hair?
Why bother to dress?
I want to be beautiful
only for him.

What use to close him
from my waking mind
when he fills my dreams.

If only
I could put an end to
"if only."

About to visit friends
I ask myself
why.

Not that the light of the moon
ever depended on you
but now that you're gone . . .

How much of the past
must be carried
into the future?

To ponder or speak
about the truth of our flesh
would be unbearable now.

For a moment
I think I understand
and feel a silent, sad peace.

This tiny mirror we shared
lies face down covered with dust
—your name written upon it.

If it's really done
why do I spend night after night
writing poems to him?

This evening breeze
brings a sorrow
older than he and I.

Days go by
when I do not
speak his name.

I give myself to another
receive pleasure
without joy.

I know he will never return
yet each night
I leave a light burning.

So many poems for him
but I do not even know
where he is.

Joy left my life
when he did.
I keep telling myself
winter is only ninety-one days.

So much lost already
I can't wait
for this year to be over.

Why do I record all this
when he will never
see a word of it?

I no longer remember
what he looks like
but the blood does not forget.

Not yet, not yet
but the day will come
when I do not think of you.

The edges around sleep
filled with secrets
that tear the heart.

All these poems
that arrive with the darkness
—only the ashes

Each day I awake
with the hope it'll be gone
—this dull ache in the heart.

Because I have nothing else
I have begun to love
my sorrow.

No matter what the news
it remains another day
without you.

The silence before the dawn:
may it enter
my heart.

I sent the poems to a long time poetic comrade, John Brandi, in New Mexico. His response was strong and immediate. He wanted to do a few drawings to accompany them and then, if possible, get them out into the world. He showed them to Linnea Gentry at Amaranth Press and, in partnership with Tooth of Time, the result was an elegant little chapbook with five of John's hand colored illustrations. It was titled *Only the Ashes*, limited to two hundred copies, most of which went to friends of those involved in the enterprise with the exception of a few which were sent to poets in Japan. There was a vague and wild hope that a copy might somehow reach Kage or that someone would translate them back into Japanese.

The response was slow and quiet, sort of like the poems.

A few questions. A few compliments. Some mild criticism. Through the years an occasional query: How could Kage be reached? Where was she now? Who was she really? Did it actually happen like that? In the flesh? In the mind? In a dream? Did it happen at all?

The motel was the Fox Motel on Highway 11E between Jonesborough and Johnson City. The roadside cafe was actually a pizza joint, now long gone. And Kage? Kage was herself—a presence, a voice, a spirit, a vehicle for words that flow through the heart, a muse if you will.

For centuries poets have spoken of, dreamed of, invoked the muse—each of us in our own way. For some she resembles Robert Graves' White Goddess. For others she's closer to Edmund Schaeffer's Divine Woman of the Far East. For still others it's been Lilith with all the attending danger or the Fox Women of Japan or, most probably, our own mates and lovers.

Regardless of the form, what ultimately matters is how she is received. What will she say? Will we hear it? Will we remember it? The point is to be prepared to receive the gift however and in whatever form it comes, just as keeping his mind focused all those years, Hsiang-Yen (Japanese—Kyôgen) was ready when a pebble from the path he was sweeping plinked against a bamboo and opened his mind/heart to the enlightenment he had so long sought.

While the cranes were heading south in the autumn of 1995, a small packet arrived in my mailbox with no return address, just a postmark from Williamsburg, Virginia. Inside, on separate sheets of paper, were these poems:

Thank you
for enough
to move on

The poems reached me:
were they really mine
or what you needed?

America—
you and
that pizza

There were a few
but on this summer night
only cold memories

Too much time
trying to replace
what was good

Two years
a nun
— a useless exercise

That butterfly
dead from the cold
— my youthful dreams

Once again they were signed *Kage.*

There is a long tradition among poets and singers to speak
through the voices of others or have others speak through
them. The Dragon Woman of the Luminous Moon Pool sang
her quatrains through the T'ang poet Ho Kuang-yuan. At the
end of the nineteenth century, the Scottish critic and essayist,
William Sharp, used Fiona Macleod's romantic novels and
poems to eloquently express what otherwise would have

remained unsaid. And closer to our own time, "a contemporary young woman who lives near the temple of Marishi-ben in Kyôto," adopted the pen name of Marichiko and allowed Kenneth Rexroth to bring forth some of his sweetest and most passionate lyrics.

I once heard a story about Kenneth attending a conference on Asian poetry in Japan. At one of the sessions, a scholar took the floor and chastised him about his mistranslation of some phrase in one of Marichiko's poems. Rexroth gently tried to defend himself, when another scholar rose to back up the first. Rexroth quietly said they were entitled to their opinion but he was going to let the poems stand as they were.

Thus far no one has told me that the translations of Kage are wrong.

CROCUSES IN THE SNOW

—for Sarah

to shake all morning
because you touched me
—a simple bow

fighting sleep
to prolong
the sweetness

like a new season
she stands between me
and old sorrows

by the refrigerator light
her bending body
through a new kimono

each time
surprised by it:
beauty beyond desire

her perfect breasts
—two pulsing birds
in my hands

after all these years
her panties on the floor
still do it for me

not washing
just to taste her
all day long

shut in by winter rain
we come close
and know each other

limbs entangled
we dream
each other's dream

a petal falls
     you
across the table

this love
a continual revelation
—crocuses in the snow

Edith Shiffert

Yama-Biko: Mountain Echo

Forty years looking
up at the eastern mountain
not high, not far, here!

For forty years I have lived directly below Mt. Hiei on the east side of the ancient city of Kyôto. Twenty four of these years have been shared with my husband, Minoru, hiking nearby and in the Japanese mountains, both of us writing poems, short and long. We traveled yearly overseas for several months visiting my family and seeing new places.

Aging, we continued to walk along the streamside path

known as the Philosopher's Walk. Here we enjoyed being with the birds on the Takano and Kamo rivers, feeding the pigeons and sparrows. We spent hours with the elegant herons and the tame seagulls which gathered here for the mild winters. Our lives were full and thoughtful.

Then, when I was eighty-six and Minoru ninety-one, our wonderful life changed. Minoru's developing Alzheimers and my opsteoporosis meant we could no longer care for ourselves. A retirement home was found in the historic and scenic area of Ohara on the other side of Mt. Hiei. Since August 2002, we have made our new home Yama-Biko, or Mountain Echo.

> Roofed with heavy clouds
> and veiled in the shifting mists
> Mountain Echo home.

> Stillness comes out from
> solitary depths inside
> steep cedar forests.

The small mountains all around us are mostly covered with cedar trees. We used to hike in them but now we cannot even step off a paved path. Flowering trees and shrubs keep the slopes colorful more than half the year. Plum and cherry blossoms, azaleas and rhododendrons, hydrangeas, morning glory and wisteria.

Those flower petals
from roots in earth, stems in light!
Self too roots and lifts.

From the first we were aware of a pair of hawks in their lookout tower by the rice fields and vegetable farms bordering our complex. We feel they are conscious of us and share our existence.

Abiding with hawks
we also know the long rains
and when sunrise comes.

After the typhoon
a bird chirping and chirping
where none was before.

We too watch darkness
slowly descend over fields
and silence widen.

Hawks from their tower
above deep snow this morning
soar up, swoop down, up.

I am conscious of all the changes of day and night, and the seasons, and do not feel lonely, even though there are no English speakers among the residents and staff here.

The way of those hawks,
we watch and when they fly up
it seems we do too.

In the winter there is snow almost every day but it usually
melts by mid-morning. Beautiful to look at or have falling on
us.

The plum flowers bloom
in the snowstorms's new whiteness
though I have not changed.

Like heavy snowfall
piled fragrant along branches
flowers melt away.

The Buddha body
growing in my own body,
in that cedar tree?

In season we are attentive to insects and frogs. Bright
green frogs, the size of a fingernail, settle onto a balcony
flower box and several even come inside for several days.
Sitting on our balcony we watch evening fading to darkness
and the darting flashes of many fireflies. The pleasure and
interest we feel sharing our lives with all these non-humans,
even a tiny firefly, is sufficient to ease our sorrows. We feel
fortunate to be here though it is not the lifestyle we would

have chosen. No more travel to Hawaii, Hong Kong, California, Alaska, Macao, or even the Japanese mountains and shores. But it is quiet, peaceful, safe, and we are content. We know who and what we are even while we endure our final mental and physical transformations. I have sufficient solitude to realize whatever can be known is what I have sought as a follower of the Asian hermit poet tradition.

> As if conversing
> the harsh voice of a lone crow
> comes from the forest.

> These solitary
> silences I sometimes find
> give satisfaction.

Yama-Biko has several paved paths I can still manage to walk on, taking no more than a twenty minute walk. But to walk daily throughout the seasons is to witness endless changes all interlinked with the time, my condition, and the facts of existence. It becomes an experience of the interconnection of all things, their cycles, the accidents, the evolving evolution on, under, and over the earth's surfaces, and beyond. My husband and I are confined but there are no barriers to our experience of the most simple and varied things.

> Tree of my spirit
> within me all my lifetime,
> can its roots still spread?

This winter sunlight
on the tallest cedar tips,
on the small mountains.

On Mt. Hiei
the New Year snow has fallen.
Cold and silent night.

Even before the snows end there is a succession of tiny
flowers covering the ground. Little blue veronica opens its
ground-covering patches of tiny flowers, morning after
morning for months, often surrounded by snow. The trees
and shrubs, in the garden and in nature, succeed each other
in waves of colorful, sometimes fragrant, blossoms.

Their meditation
or mine, clustered blue flowers
of hydrangeas?

The color purple—
Hydrangeas from June rains
dripping while they glow.

These still red thistles
where butterflies perch in mists
and white moths have feasts!

Each one a quiet
meditation—purple blue
wet hydrangeas.

Here the wildflowers are blooming out in the countryside
but I just know their Engish names. The same varieties as
over much of the earth. How could I become homesick dur-
ing two years in Alaska when the dandelions suddenly
appeared everywhere?

Two months we have watched
for plum blossoms to open.
Now already gone.

Bitter wind today
but an early violet
January's end.

Dark and light, sweet sounds
from crickets and soaring hawks.
A hundred eons?

These flocks of small birds
suddenly arriving here—
did they have a plan?

As we wander through
the eternal loneliness,
its births and its deaths!

Haiku poets, as all poets, should feel free to use the haiku in whatever way seems appropriate to their creativity. There never were any rules, just fashions and preferences. To be somewhere and write about it, that is what haiku is. You may write one hundred in a night or one in a lifetime. The history of haiku and its poets, as with many things, is endlessly fascinating but is no substitute for the creative response to the moment.

White veils on the hills
appear and vanish again.
Ohara spring mists.

The whole landscape goes
and then breaks thru from the mists
pouring down Mt. Hiei.

Still the same mountain
but now from the other side
as I near ninety.

In the great emptiness of my 88th year
plum flowers in a snowstorm, and I find
I'm not lonely or afraid.

At lunch that hum? A resident snoring?
Wind in a ventilator shaft?
A Buddhist priest chanting a sutra?

With whom shall I drink this tea;
the cat, Li Po's moon, or just myself?
We are all pleasant company.

In all directions
small mountains hiding the view
while being the view.

September 15, 2003

The new year begins
with the same sun overhead
and the same hiyo-bird.

That Zen monk also
nine months inside his mother.
Salted plum with rice.

In these ditches too
fallen petals of cherries,
the outcastes' district.

The lake lies quiet
between the forested hills.
Purple azaleas.

Is this joy senile?
Let be, let be, no matter.
Another new moon!

The pain of the world
not washed away by rivers
nor blown off by winds.

Oh I am zestful
in this field of grasses
openmouthed for rain.

Seen for eighty years
but still I feel awed and glad—
white water lilies.

The departed cat
still seems to be everywhere
as he was before.

Not being a monk
but feeling as though I were,
without a belief.

All I can say,
I see and am satisfied.
Big mountain. Dark night.

Resting on the earth
who needs *satori* or faith
Embrace what holds you!

With the autumn leaves
a butterfly too is blown
across our pathway.

Home from the market
I realize that my teeth
are still on the shelf.

Be still now, be still.
See the sunlight on your hands
and on air, your breath.

Carefully the cat
steps onto the snowy walk.
Darkness and whiteness!

On my final walk
I look carefully for
whatever is there.

You and you and you
I have known intimately.
Just this feeling left.

CONTRIBUTORS NOTES

JOHN BRANDI is a poet, writer, artist, and traveler. He is the author of more than thirty six books of poetry, essays, and haiku. His most recent collection of poems is *In What Disappears.* His journeys have carried him to Southeast Asia, India, the Himalayas, Indonesia, Mexico, and Cuba. He has made his home in New Mexico since 1971, most recently in El Rito.

MARGARET CHULA lived in Kyoto, Japan, for twelve years, where she taught creative writing and studied woodblock printing and ikebana. She is the author of a number of volumes of poetry including *Grinding My Ink; This Moment; Always Filling, Always Full;* and *The Smell of Rust.* Active in the international haiku community, she now makes her home in Portland, Oregon.

CID CORMAN was the editor of the seminal magazine *Origin.* A prolific poet, translator, and editor, he lived abroad most of his adult life, first in Europe and then in Kyoto, Japan. His most recent books include *The Famous Blue Aerogrammes* and a reprint of his translation of Bashô's travel journal, *Back Roads to Far Towns.* He died in 2004.

DIANE DIPRIMA is one of the most important poets of the Beat generation. During the late '50s and early '60s she lived in Manhattan but for the past thirty-five years she has lived in Northern California. She is a student of Zen and Tibetan

Buddhism, Sanskrit, and alchemy. She has published over thirty-five books including *Revolutionary Letters, Loba, Pieces of a Song: Selected Poems,* and her autobiographic memoir, *Recollections of My Life as a Woman.*

PATRICIA DONEGAN is the author of *Without Warning, Heralding the Milk Light,* and *Hot Haiku.* She is the translator of *Chiyo-ni: Woman Haiku Master* (with Yoshie Ishibashi). She teaches in Tokyo, Japan, and is the poetry editor of *Kyoto Journal.*

PENNY HARTER is a poet and teacher. Her sixteen books include *Turtle Blessings, Lizard Light: Poems From the Earth,* and *Buried in the Sky.* She is also the co-author of the *Haiku Handbook: How to Write, Share, and Teach Haiku.*

CHRISTOPHER HEROLD was a student of Shunryu Suzuki Roshi and wrote his first haiku in 1968 during an early practice session at the Tassajara Zen Center. He has worked as a drummer and a gardener. His books of haiku include *In Other Words, Coincidence,* and *A Path in the Garden.* He is the editor of the international haiku journal, *The Heron's Nest.*

WILLIAM J. HIGGINSON is a leading expert on haiku as well as a poet and translator. He is the author and editor of several major haiku texts including T*he Haiku Seasons: Poetry of the Natural World* and *The Haiku Handbook: How to Write, Share, and Teach Haiku.* His own books of poems include *Healing and Other Poems, Paterson Pieces, Death Is* and *Approaches to the Edge.*

Elizabeth Searle Lamb was a founding member of the Haiku Society of America in 1968, served as its president, and for many years as editor of *Frogpond,* its magazine. She has won more than 150 awards for her haiku and her work has been translated into several languages. She is the author of a number of collections of haiku, the bulk of which were gathered together in her last book, *Across the Harp: Collected and New Haiku,* published in 1999. She died in 2004.

Michael McClure has published over thirty books, including most recently *Rain Mirror* and *Plum Stones.* A key figure in the San Francisco renaissance of the '50s, he currently performs with Doors' keyboardist Ray Manzarek and continues to push the boundaries of literary possibilities.

Sonia Sanchez is a poet, activist, and scholar. She is the author of many collections of poetry including *Does Your House Have Lions, Like the Singing Coming off the Drum,* and *Shake Loose My Skin: New and Selected Poems.*

Steve Sanfield is a poet who makes his home in the foothills of the Sierra Nevada Mountains in California. He is the author of a number of volumes of poems including *A New Way, In One Year and Out the Other, Only the Ashes,* and *Crocuses in the Snow.*

Edith Shiffert has lived in Kyoto, Japan since 1963. She is the author of eleven collections of poetry, including several volumes of haiku. Her most recent volume is *Pathways.* She has also translated several volumes of poetry from the Japanese, including Haiku Master Buson.

ACKNOWLEDGMENTS

(Continued from copyright page)

John Brandi—"Trigger of Light" first appeared in *Kyoto Journal* and some of the haiku first appeared in *Weeding the Cosmos: Selected Haiku*, La Alemeda Press, 1994. Reprinted by permission of the author.

Margaret Chula—Some of the haiku appeared in *Grinding My Ink*, 1993, and *The Smell of Rust*, 2003, both published by Katsura Press. Reprinted by permission of the author.

Cid Corman—Some of these poems first appeared in the journal *Modern Haiku* and in various publications by Cid Corman published by Bob Arnold at Longhouse and are reprinted with his permission.

Patricia Donegan—"An Antidote to Speed" first appeared in *Kyoto Journal*. Reprinted by permission of the author.

Penny Harter—"Seeing and Connecting" first appeared in *Newsweek Japan*. Some of the haiku first appeared in *The Monkey's Face*, From Here Press, 1987; *Stages and Views*, Katydid Books, 1994; *Shadow Play: Night Haiku*, Simon and Schuster, 1994; and in *Frogpond*, *The Heron's Nest*, *Haijinx*, and *Haiku Southwest*. Reprinted by permission of the author.

Christopher Herold—The prose and some of the haiku

were first published in *A Path in the Garden*, Katsura Press, 2000 and other haiku first appeared in the following: *Acorn, Haiku Anthology of America Members Anthology, In the Margins of the Sea, Woodnotes, Modern Haiku, Haiku Moment, Morning Snow,* the *Ueno Basho Anthology,* and *Red Moon Anthology.* Reprinted by permission of the author.

William J. Higginson—"Santa Fe Shopping Carts" first appeared in *Modern Haiku.* Some of the haiku first appeared in *Ten Years Collected Haiku,* From Here Press,1987; *Etudes for Eastre,* From Here Press, 1972; *Cycling Patterson,* Sea Ox, 1974, and in *Haiku, The Haiku Anthology, Haiku Highlights, Harvest, Mann Library Daily Hiaku, Tinywords.com,* and *Dream Wanderer.* Reprinted by permission of the author.

Elizabeth Searle Lamb—Some of the haiku appeared in the *Basho Festival Haiku Anthology,* and *Across the Windharp: Collected and New Haiku,* La Alameda Press, 1999. Reprinted by permission of the author's estate.

Sonia Sanchez—Some of the haiku were previously published and are reprinted by permission of the author.

Steve Sanfield—"Only the Ashes" was originally published by Tooth of Time Books and the haiku were first published in *Crocuses in the Snow,* Tangram Press. Reprinted by permission of the author.

Edith Shiffert—Some of the haiku first appeared in *The Light Comes Slowly*, Katsura Press, 1997. Reprinted by permission of the author.

Companions for the Journey Series

This series presents inspirational work by well-known writers
in a small-book format designed to be carried along
on your journey through life.

Volume 8
The Unswept Path
Contemporary American Haiku
Edited by John Brandi and Dennis Maloney
1-893996-38-7   5 X 7 $15.00

Volume 7
Lotus Moon
The Poetry of Rengetsu
Translated by John Stevens
Afterword by Bonnie Myotai Treace
1-893996-36-0   5 x 7   132 pages $14.00

Volume 6
A Zen Forest: Zen Sayings
Translated by Soioku Shigematsu
Preface by Gary Snyder
1-893996-30-1   5 x 7   140 pages $14.00

Volume 5
Back Roads to Far Towns
Basho's Travel Journal
Translated by Cid Corman
1-893996-31-X   5 x 7   128 pages $13.00

Volume 4

Heaven My Blanket, Earth My Pillow
Poems from Sung Dynasty China by Yang Wan-Li
Translated by Jonathan Chaves
1-893996-29-8   5 x 7   120 pages $14.00

Volume 3

10,000 Dawns
The Love Poems of Claire and Yvan Goll
Translated by Thomas Rain Crowe and Nan Watkins
1-893996-27-1   5 x 7   96 pages $13.00

Volume 2

There Is No Road
Proverbs by Antonio Machado
Translated by Mary G. Berg & Dennis Maloney
1-893996-66-2   5 x 7   120 pages $14.00

Volume 1

Wild Ways: Zen Poems of Ikkyu
Translated by John Stevens
1-893996-65-4   5 x 7   128 pages $14.00